My Grandma and Grandpa

MB
MACAW
BOOKS

© Macaw Books

www.macawbooks.com

Printed in India

Coco and Polly loved visiting their grandparents' house. Polly loved to be in the kitchen when Grandma was cooking.

How yummy everything smelled! Polly loved to watch Grandma cook. Grandma always cooked her whatever she asked for. Being with grandma was always a treat!

Grandma knitted wonderful sweaters for her grandchildren. This time, she had knitted a nice green muffler and a cosy red jumper for Polly. 'Ooh! This will keep me warm all winter!' said Polly, happily. And grandma had made mittens for Polly's cat Fluffy too! 'Now Fluffy will not be cold either!' said Polly.

Grandma always told Polly bedtime stories. Often Polly listened to the stories in Grandma's lap and drifted off to sleep. Then Grandma would gently tuck the little girl into bed. 'Good night, my darling,' Grandma always said, kissing Polly on the forehead. Polly always had sweet dreams in Grandma's bed.

Polly loved her grandpa too. His snoring shook the whole house!
It woke Polly up every morning.

He loved to do magic tricks too.
He would sit in his big armchair in
the living room and do his tricks.

His teeth are fake, one is made of gold,

Grandpa must be a hundred years old!

100

13

The children loved to go on picnics with their grandparents. Grandma's picnic basket was always full of tasty snacks. They spread their picnic blanket, and snacked happily on the grass.

We love them more and more as we grow
Oh, we love grandma and grandpa so!

My brothers
and sisters

Selena had three brothers, and three sisters.
Their house was always noisy and happy.

Someone was always being naughty,
and someone was always setting
them right. How much it was to have
so many brothers and sisters!

Selena's twin sister Tina was her friend. They did everything together. The two girls loved to wear the same clothes and look exactly like each other.

Selena and Tina loved to trick people. Selena often pretended to be Tina, and Tina pretended to be Selena. What a laugh they always had!

Their elder brother Otto loved to give the girls piggyback rides. The girls squealed with delight as they looked down from their elder brother's shoulders.

Otto loved to cook as well! He loved to make snacks for his sisters. He often baked them cookies and made them sandwiches. 'Yumm!' said Tina, as she bit into a sandwich.

Tessa was the girls' elder sister. She walked them to school every day, and picked them back up as well. The girls loved to tell her stories of what happened at school.

After school, Tessa took Selena and Tina to the swimming pool. The girls always had so much fun splashing about in the water!

Their eldest sister Rosie loved to play pranks on the girls. One day, she hid herself inside Selena and Tina's cupboard. Then she waited for the girls to reach their room.

Later, when Tina and Selena sat by their dressing table and brushed their hair, she called out in a spooky voice, 'Booo! Booo! The ghost is coming to get youuuuuu!' Selena and Tina were so afraid that they ran out of their room screaming, 'Ghost! Ghost!'

Selena was always angry at their brother Dennis because he always ate their cookies. But he also made her smile by telling her funny jokes.

Dennis, Selena and Tina always made a huge ruckus playing pranks on each other. The three of them were the jokers of the family.

Their youngest brother was a baby. They called him Little Bill. Selena and Tina loved to rock his cradle and sing to him.

'Cooo!' said Little Bill, happily, when he saw his brothers and sisters. How they all loved Little Bill!

With seven children, there was never a dull moment in the house. 'I love having a big family!' Selena often said. And it was true, for a large, noisy family was always a fun family!

www.ingramcontent.com/pod-product-compliance
Lightning Source LLC
LaVergne TN
LVHW082324080426

835508LV00042B/1530